DEVIKA'S POETIC GALLERY

DEVIKA DHYANI

Made with ♥ on the Notion Press Platform
www.notionpress.com

Devika's Poetic Gallery

Contents

Contents

Foreword

A vision with a thought, a vision with wings, a vision with colours is the way I describe my poems. My poems will be enjoyed by my readers as a blend of emotions, expressions and feelings.

Preface

The very base for coming up with writing of English poetry is my love towards English literature. To express my approach, my outlook towards diversified topics, vivid areas of interest I found the medium of poetic expressions as the most impressive.

Acknowledgements

I extend my sincere thanks to the nature of environment as well as the variety of human nature

Prologue

<u>First Edition</u>

Chapter1

Nature all around

Mountains Rivers Oceans

Are no less than emotions

Valleys Tides Waves

Are the faces of grace

Is enfolded with artistry

And is inbound within symmetry

Encourages all kind with its beauty

To serve, strengthen and nurture as one duty

To make human admires the nature

Learns to love and love to live with same gesture

As we boost our love for all kind

We are showered with bliss filled with love as we find

Chapter2

Rains

Rains in form of water drops

Are the base, the ace that crops

Rains inside leads to an enlightenment that glow

Rains outside leads to a rainbow that show

Rains purifies the environment

As it delights the apparent

Rains are desired Rains are required

Rains are the best as forms the best

Which is static is as aesthetic ; is form of zest

Chapter3

Love for TATA

Offices and offices are surrounding but with no bonding

Concerned with their wealth but least with employee's
health

Some are big in name some are small in fame

But are one and same for the concern of humane

Amidst such approach we have our sovereign

Who is the finest in all kind

With employee prosperity as prime focus in mind

Is none other but our very own benign

Forms a prestigious group alike a family

Whom we proudly call One TATA One family

Chapter4

Teacher

Teacher TeacherTeacher
With a transformed feature
Reflects in incredible ability of boss
Who is a substantial gross
Advise, mentor and promote
So that we grow as a one thought
This is a leadership quality of our boss
Who directs, supports and endorse

Chapter5

Independence

Independence is not a word but a thought which is much sought

Independence is not a word but a thought for which we fought

Independence leads to a building of nation

Which is vivid diversified but still enroute to one station

Independence needs the unanimous consent of free citizens

To fight against vicious and build nation with perfection

To make India's Independence growth significant

We should move towards one ethical advisement

To build corruption-free, environment-friendly, peaceful nation

Chapter6

We

Hear the music of the band, see the beauty of the land
From the mountain to the sand, this nation of our is sure grand
As the culture of vivid states, is diverse in ways
Alike the notes of sonnets , is alluring blend which says
We the gals and guys as teammates, are the hope of rays
Not only of our organization, but of the whole nation

Chapter7

EversomeCleversome

Ways are copious and approaches numerous

Goals are precise with essence of spice

Some starts clever and ends up never

Some are sly whose honesty never apply

But always rely the one who comply; for whom limit is
the sky

Ethics, loyalty, manners are bestowed with luck

Unlike shrewd and clever who are defamed and morally
suck

Still some are clever and corrupt ; and are fully inept

and remains and remains eversomecleversome inside and
out

Chapter8

Love Ditty
My amorous love, My arch-desire
My Cinthia,
You, the aurora of my love
the apex of my temptation
Your passionate love is an
antidote to my desperate madness
Love is never antagonistic, hostile
or atrocious
But is always audacious and
magnanimous

Chapter9

The Passion – revealed

Lover's heart, a vast ocean

Layers of senses are in motion

Sometimes tranquil, sometimes tumult

Emerging from the inner cult

As love superannuated, is sacramental

With the gist of contractual,

As, union of body and soul

Chapter10

Divine Love
Presence of cupid here,
Is enclosed within one sphere
Veracious presence which is ratified,
But, subtle to be personified
Is the odium against that sheer love,
Which is flippering amid numerous hearts,
Also, amid the numerous flowers ;
To rise and kiss that Divine Love

Chapter11

You – my beloved
You, and your thoughts sustains a part,
of my bounding heart
A heart, brooded and appareled,
in your love, my beloved
Your love is to me a celestial cataract,
accentuating the intensity of my heart infact
My heart saturated with your love,
is but a sky at dusk covered with doves

Chapter12

You and I
You and I in each others embrace
Climbing together, rungs of faith
Are kissing, depths of love 'n' senses
Senses emerging from your heart and entering mine
Are as authentic as a reign
My heart, apart from the vagaries of reign
Is enclosed in the eyes of thine
The eyes which are abode of mine

Chapter13

Thy Love
Nay, it's not a quatrain,
but a perpetual fact
Blooming like rosemary,
like cear sacrosanct
Benign to begin with,
probity persist
Rife like life,
unique like sentiment
Power of my life,
is-thy love

Chapter14

Thou

Thou as vital as vitality
My feelings yield for thy fidelity
Longing to be thy side forever
Confined in thine arms now and forever
Is the dream, endeavor or ardour
Whichis a faith and fervor
Filled with trust ever and ever

Chapter15

Variety of people
People having classification as vivid
Are with approach and attitude rigid
Are clever having nature shrewd
With words and language as rude
Some are sweeter with inside bitter
Some are clever and are genuine never
Talks about unity with belief in duality
Are super sly in reality

Chapter16

<u>Second Edition</u>

Chapter17

Independence

Independence is a way
Where rights and ethics stay
Where we have our say
Where sunshine brightens our way
With a hope of ray
Not only on a single day
But every moment we pray
Independence is a feel
With the spirit of zeal
That nourishes and heal
Independence is complete
With a sense of discrete
Having a blend of concrete

Chapter18

Organisation

Diamond in a jewel
or a pearl in a snail
Is a dwelling where
love and positivity prevail
Working with ethics
progressing with statics
Makes TCE a leader
among its competitors
Leads to successfulness
with gist of happiness
With the team mission
makes its global vision
Is the art is the focus
and the learning
Which proudly we call
our way of working

Chapter19

Love for nature

Love around your sphere
And the faith you access
Is like the aura in the air
Alike the wisdom you posses
Blooming flowers and chirping birds
Burbling cataracts or vast oceans
Make us ecstatic as we heard
And arouse our very emotions
Dreamy clouds amid endless sky
Magnificent rainbow and sparkling dews
Make us euphoric to ply
With the approach absolutely new
Nature and love are as allied
As tide is with another tide

Chapter 20

Mr and Mrs Fox

People have vivid types of nature
And are made of various arts
That forms the basis of their character
And make their conspiracy starts
They says something and acts another
Busy making self made story
Cooks and crooks and narrates together
And makes an interesting allegory
Such people are so wicked
And holds an entire team
That their every move is picked
But shows the relations seam
Such are the variety of hoax
That the people call Mr and Mrs Fox

Chapter21

Liers

Liers around we have ample
With one or more sample
Some lie the work they do
And try to make people woo
Some lie the fame they possess
And exaggerate what otherwise is less
Some lie the trivial matters
And make relations scatter
Some lie the source of treasure
And are only interested in their pleasure
The unmatched is to lie the name
And plays the cunning game
To project their social rank frame

Chapter22

Respect

Respect is a thought and a feel

Which flourishes within us and heal

Respect is a love and a care

With whom emotions we share

The maximum we have respect for others

The minimum we have grudges from others

Surrounding is special

With respect at every level

And for human and its survival

Chapter23

Bribe takers

Bribe takers are the shakers

Of the pride and glory of our nation makers

Bribe takers accrue more and more bribe

Builds their mansion and subscribe

Not to the traits of responsible citizen

But are immoral and anti-national in their actions

Such low graded people should be expelled

All their wealth should be held

To be a lesson and learning for bribe takers

And to be a motivation for ethical nation makers

Chapter24

War

War is such a state

Where humanity has no gate

War leads to destruction

With no motive of construction

We should talk, chat and converse

And should not get unfriendly or adverse

We should have internal war against our faults and indiscretion

And should have external war against cunning and corruption

We should have war with approach for reducing pollution

And providing nation a solution

Chapter25

Captain Hook and Mrs Crook
Captain Hook and Mrs Crook
Together they plan and cook
Hook is always in disguise
Crook playing shrewd and wise
Hook and Crook hands in hand
Conspire desire in the band
Hook in himself is cunning and clever
But is diminishing as compared to partner
Hook and Crook cooks and cook
Lot of tricks with innocent look

Chapter26

Liars Love

Love your name
but don't play a game
Love your caste
but don't make falsehood last
Love your family to be happier
but don't betray your familiar
Love your goals
but don't betray others in a whole
Love your passion
but don't make fooling others a fashion

Chapter27

Education
Education is not about mere literate
but to spread love and ignore hate
Education teach us to be skilled
and to make our dreams fulfilled
Education reflects in our action
which is our true inner reflection
Education makes us more refined
and makes our morals and ethics defined
Education is indispensable and integral
which makes human independent and Imperial

Chapter28

Romanticism

Romanticism of water for cataract is phenomenal
together the ardor they possess is for real
Passion amid flowers and butterflies is substantial
together they embellish the circumferential
Rainbow reflects the vibrant colours in the sky
allied the emblazon beauty of nature they intensify
Mountains embrace the huge radiant sky
together they make the environment beautify
Flowers,Cataracts,Mountains,Climate and Sky
together they make abode for dreams to fly

Chapter29

Honest poverty Dishonest wealth

Honesty is the needy's wealth

as corruption is a part of opportunist health

Poor make their way with honest needs

Opportunist make their way with corrupt deeds

Poor earns fame with their honest name

Opportunist change their name for the false game

Poor works hard and earns wage

Opportunist acts unfair and receives bribe at every stage

Poverty with still honest approach is appreciable

Opportunist with pure immoral thought is bribable

Chapter30

Flowers

Flowers with a dew
alike humane with awe
are one in a few
Flowers have petals
which are not metals
but makes our jungle settles
Flowers amid self incense
seems beautiful in every lens
are motivating to every sense
Flowers feed fly and bee
is as pure as we see
promotes ecosystem actively
Flowers are bouquet of affection
that shows in every reflection
and is our way of selection

Chapter31

Essential luxury

Essentials were food cloth and shelter
are now changed to luxury in the centre
Essentials were the bare minimum provision
to live life with value and vision
But now the essentials are the luxury
with it's very own importance and priority
In this race to gather and procure luxury
we are overlooking our sincerity
Luxury should not be sought
with the value and ethics as its cost
but our essential need should be bought